Overleaf: (l) Stars Over the Umpqua

To my wife, Carolyn, and
our son, Parker.
Two generous souls who
are always "looking up."

Night Skies
by Paul Alan Bennett

Copyright © 2018

All rights reserved under the Pan-American and International Copyright Commission

First Edition

No part of this book may be reproduced without the written permission of the author, Paul Alan Bennett.

ISBN: 978-0-578-41042-5

Several of the images are available as
12" by 18" prints and 5" by 7" blank greeting cards.
Go to paulalanbennett.com

Special thanks to Sally Sundsten at Ideas to Inks,
DeeAnn Glazier at Xpress Printing and Dennis McGregor
for their design assistance.

Also, thank-you to Leslie Lawrence, Rob Corrigan,
Carol Dixon, Helen Schmidling, Curtiss Abbott
and the Bend Art Center
for their contributions.

Overleaf: (2) Constellations over the Lava Fields

NIGHT SKIES

by Paul Alan Bennett

*To Terry —
Keep looking up!
Paul Alan Bennett*

Look up! Look up at the night sky.

(4) Stars over the High Desert

Look up. Feel the wonder and mystery above you.

(5) Driving Back from Redmond at Night

Take a moment. See the lights of the constellations and the planets.
See the quiet movement of airplanes and satellites.

(6) October Skies

Feel the earth rotating, the stars circling in space.

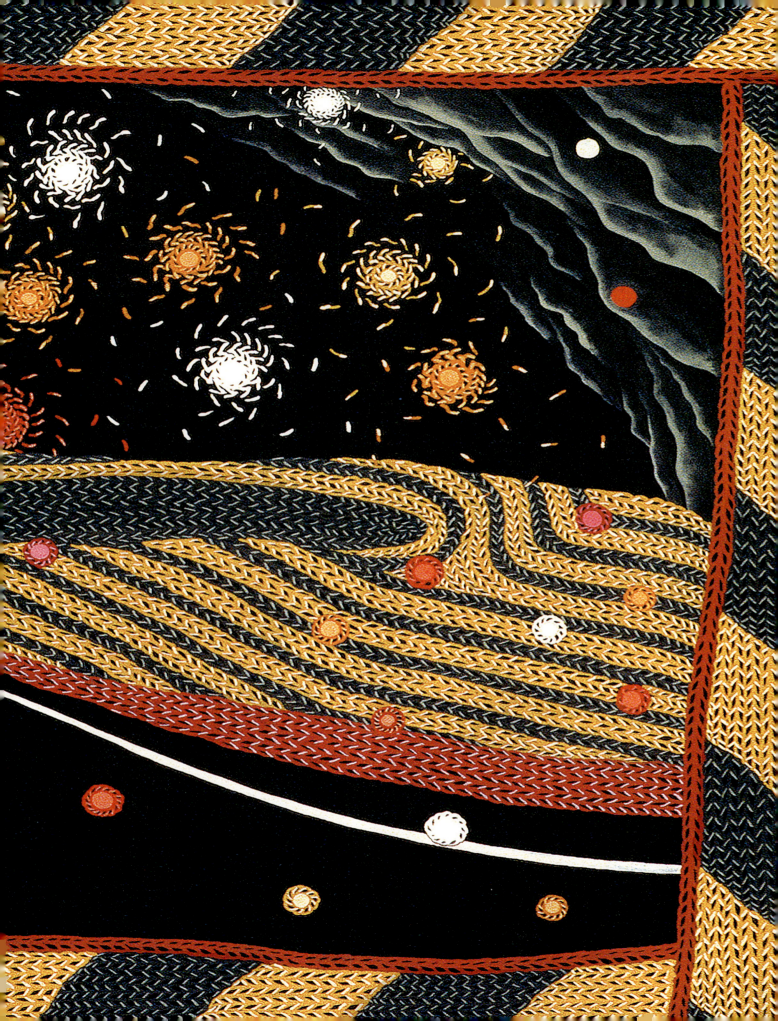

Overleaf: (7) Stardust Everywhere South of The Dalles

(8) Echoes in the Cascades

Feel the moon welcoming your gaze.

Feel the night upon your skin.

Imagine yourself following a moonbeam on a paddle board!

(IO) Paddle Boarding Under Virgo Skies

Or chasing the reflection of the stars of Libra.

Inhale deeply and slowly exhale the universe.

Embrace this beauty with a thousand arms.

Use your deeper senses.

Overleaf: (12) Moon River

(16) Stars Over Sisters

See the forms of the landscape caressed by moonlight.

(17) Beyond Words

Watch the light bounce upon the water's surface. Listen for the beat.

(19) Waxing Moon and Gemini Skies

Remember learning the terms "waxing and waning" and how it pleased you?

Overleaf: (18) Strumming the Jet Stream

(20) Kayaking under Orion's Belt

Remember when you first recognized Orion's Belt and the Big Dipper?
They can soon feel like old friends.

(21) The Time Traveler

Be guided by moonlight dancing near the water's edge.

(22) Heartbeat

Trust that you are part of this illumination.

(23) Full Moon and Scorpio Nights

"I am a Scorpio," you say proudly.

(24) Salmon Returning under Piscean Skies

"And I am a Pisces," comes the equally proud response.
How quickly we identify with the stars!

(25) Blue Dusk with the Constellation of Cancer

The darkness of nightfall can turn the familiar world into a mysterious landscape.

Overleaf: (26) Cassiopeia over the Ochocos

(27) Pegasus Rising

Remember the stories of the constellations? Remember snake-haired Medusa whose lifeless body gave birth to the beautiful winged horse, Pegasus?

Remember sad-eyed Hercules pursuing the golden apples guarded by the 100-headed dragon?

(28) Kayaking under the Constellation of Leo

Overleaf: (29) The Constellation of Cygnus over Smith Rock

(30) Rock Climber under the Draco Constellation

Remember when Hercules slew the lion as the first of his 12 labors?

(31) Super Moon under Aquarian Skies

Blessings to the waters of Aquarius and the wheatfields of Virgo.

(32) Kayaking under The Big Dipper

Blessings to the stars in the Big Dipper pointing to Polaris, guiding travelers to known and foreign places.

Overleaf: (33) The Dance of Hercules

(34) Sailing to Andromeda

Blessings to Perseus rescuing Andromeda
from the sea monster, Cetus.

(35) Driving under the Corona Borealis

Blessings to Dionysus joyfully tossing the wedding crown of Ariadne into the night sky, it's curving pattern of stars creating the Corona Borealis.

(36) Kayaking under Sagittarian Skies

Blessings to the healing powers of the night sky.
To the life-saving skills of Chiron, the centaur.

(37) Driving under the Phoenix Constellation

To the restorative powers of the Phoenix.

(38) The Constellation of Ophiuchus

And the medicinal skills of the god of Medicine, Asclepius.

(39) Cliff Swallow under Aries Skies

Be like a bird, a messenger between the earth and the night sky.

(40) Night Swimmer under Taurus

Swim in a sea of bio-luminescence. Be your own constellation.

Overleaf: (41) Kayaking under Capricorn Skies

(42) Rowing into the Pleiades

Journey out to find your home in the stars.

Know that, as day turns to night around
the world, others are looking up, watching,
listening, imagining, embracing,
trusting, remembering, blessing,
looking for guidance and healing,
becoming their own constellations.

(43) Forest Journey

Seek fellowship.

We are all part of this illumination.
Use your deeper senses.
Join with others.
Look up!

For further reading:

Star Finder!, DK Publishing, Penguin Random House, The Smithsonian, 2017, ISBN 978-1-4654-6475-0

D'Aulaires' Book of Greek Myths, Delecorte Press, Copyright 1962, ISBN 9780385015837

Overleaf: (44) Stars Over the Deschutes Near Warm Springs